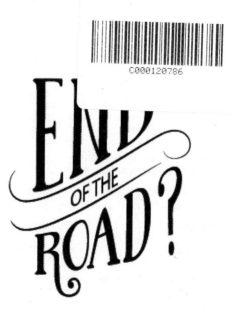

END OF THE ROAD?

Encounters with one who returned from the grave

Bible Society
Stonehill Green
Westlea
Swindon SN5 7DG
biblesociety.org.uk

First published 2018 by The British and Foreign Bible Society

ISBN: 978-0-564-04787-1

Design and production by Bible Society Resources Ltd, a wholly owned subsidiary of The British and Foreign Bible Society.

BSRL/5.3M/2019
Printed in Great Britain

CONTENTS

A MYSTERIOUS FIND

When German scholar Wilhelm Fröhner died in 1925, a marble tablet, the size of an average computer screen, was discovered at his Parisian home.

Today it belongs to the Louvre Museum, where Fröhner worked as curator. The private notes found among his belongings revealed that, in 1878, it had been sent to him from the Palestinian town of Nazareth.

The inscription on the tablet turned out to be the decree of a Roman Emperor, possibly Claudius (10BC–AD54): it said that whoever removed a dead body from a tomb would be committing a capital crime.

First century. Roman imperial edict. Grave robbery. Nazareth. Coincidence or pieces of the same puzzle?

Might, just might, Claudius, or whoever it was, have heard

of a strange sect of Christians claiming that a certain Jesus of Nazareth, executed on a Roman cross, had come back to life? Jesus, the Son of God, stronger than death, mightier than Caesar?

Suppose the Emperor concluded that Jesus' followers had robbed the corpse from the tomb before spreading the subversive rumour of his resurrection? And as the story took hold, was Rome's supreme ruler anxious to keep others from getting up to similar pranks, so much so that he threatened grave robbers with the death penalty?

The evidence is inconclusive. Nobody knows.

And yet, it is an intriguing thought. A small marble slab, shipped from Nazareth to Paris, stashed away in a secretive scholar's home: could the ancient inscription be a veiled reference to the empty tomb of Christ?

DELUDED?

Every year, people all over the world celebrate Easter as they commemorate Jesus' resurrection from the dead. 'Christ is risen,' the priest proclaims. 'He is risen indeed,' the congregation reply.

Wishful thinking, to say the least? Then again, why should raising a man from the grave be a big deal for God? Provided God exists, obviously.

But does he?

Consciously or not, people these days tend to look at the world through the lens of science. The accepted view goes something like this: science is about what we can know, whereas God is, at best, the great *un*known. We can't see him, we can't prove he is real, so bringing him into the equation adds nothing to our understanding of the world.

As science closes gap after gap in our knowledge, critics of religion wonder why anyone would want to fill the remaining gaps with a hypothetical divine being. Why not just carry on doing science, solve apparent mysteries, one by one, and leave God out of the picture?

But are things that simple? Is science fit to tell us whether God is a delusion? Is what we know about the world through science the only thing we can know? The only thing worth knowing?

Throughout history, some of the world's greatest thinkers have wrestled with the God question. That, if nothing else, should tell us it is a serious question, one that derives from other questions, like:

- Why is there not nothing?
- If the universe emerged from a quantum vacuum, why was there a quantum vacuum?
- How come anything from galaxies to microbes is governed by laws of science? Where did those laws come from? Is it scientifically established that the natural order around us is the product of chance?
- What about us humans? Can unconscious matter produce conscious beings? If we are no more than lumps of

mindless molecules, how come we keep engaging in complex musings about life, the universe and everything? And is 'love' just a chemical reaction in a physical brain?

The truth is, science can't help us with any of this. Facing our ignorance, we have two options. We can either shrug our shoulders or keep probing. Could there be a creator who set everything in motion – an 'unmoved mover', as the Greek philosopher Aristotle put it? Is there any such thing as the human spirit and, if so, does that make an Ultimate Spirit more likely?

There is another issue about which science remains silent. One day, death will put an end to our achievements, dreams, hopes and loves. Does that brute fact render life meaningless? Or might there be a point to it all, despite and beyond death?

That final question takes us right to Good Friday and Easter Sunday.

LAW AND ORDER

Ancient Judaism revolved round the Torah – the Holy Scriptures – and the temple. Year on year, Jews from all over Israel and beyond flocked to the temple in Jerusalem to celebrate the festival of Passover, commemorating their ancestors' escape from slavery in Egypt, centuries before.

During one particular Passover season, around AD30, travelling preacher Jesus of Nazareth, from the northern region of Galilee, caused a stir in the temple as he confronted the religious leaders. They didn't take kindly to this; in fact, Jerusalem's high priest, Caiaphas, ended up handing him over to the local Roman official, Pontius Pilate.

The Jewish lands had been Roman territory since Pompey the Great's conquest of Jerusalem, nearly a century earlier. The land meant a great deal to Jews, for they believed it was God's gift to them. In other words, no self-respecting Israelite would have been keen on the sound of Roman boots on their ground. But after Jesus had publicly opposed the religious leaders, they had no qualms about teaming up with the enemy.

Jesus had fired more than one dart at the heart of the religious elite. He had challenged their take on the Torah, reinterpreted the Sabbath – the holy day of rest – and questioned some of their temple practices. He was a liability. And the Romans, forever determined to keep their Empire strong and stable, disapproved of people putting the status quo at risk. In fact, they tended to execute them without much ado.

In the end, Pilate behaved no differently; he could not afford to alienate the Jewish elite who helped keep the people under control. On the day we call Good Friday, Jesus was sentenced to death, tortured, nailed to a cross and left to suffocate or bleed to death, whichever came first.

Archaeologists have unearthed two remarkable items in Israel: a stone with Pontius Pilate's name on it and an ossuary (a stone box used to house a deceased person's bones after the flesh had wasted away) bearing the name of Caiaphas – possibly the very

Caiaphas who was Jerusalem's high priest at the time of Jesus' arrest.

And so we have two historical individuals at the centre of Good Friday: a religious and a political leader. Caiaphas and Pilate. Two men so keen on law and order that their brief, fateful encounter with Jesus may have blinded them to who he really was.

WHOSE SIDE ARE YOU ON?

First-century Jews were split over how to handle their Roman overlords.

Three centuries earlier, Alexander the Great had conquered much of the known world and aimed to Hellenise it. In other words, he introduced Greek culture and language everywhere. The Bible lands were no exception.

Read the Jewish Scriptures – what Christians commonly call the Old Testament – and you'll notice that keeping away from foreign gods and customs was essential to being a Jew.

But what was, say, an upper-class Jerusalemite in the second century BC to do, if he wanted his son to succeed? No matter how much he might have clung to his own religious and cultural roots, he would have seen to it that the boy got a decent education, which meant a Greek one.

To be sure, there were those who wanted nothing to do with non-Jewish culture and religion. Others, though, were unashamedly pro-Hellenist. One Jewish high priest who, tellingly, had adopted the Greek name Jason, began to turn Jerusalem into a Greek city by authorising building projects such as a gymnasium. During the term of high priest Menelaus, the temple mount was even dedicated to Zeus-Olympus.

Two hundred years later, Jews, whose land was now occupied by the Romans, faced similar issues. Some chose to adapt to Greco-Roman culture. Some took refuge in nit-picking religious observance. Some took themselves away from what they saw as the compromising lot of Rome-pleasers and founded a religious community of their own. Others yet became guerrilla fighters and terrorists.

Where did Jesus of Nazareth and his followers figure in all of this?

One of Jesus' 'biographers', named Luke, mentions a certain Simon the Zealot among Jesus' inner circle, or disciples as the

Bible calls them. Zealots wanted to establish God's rule on earth by ousting the foreign invaders by force. And further on in what is known as Luke's Gospel we read that, on the eve of Jesus' fateful clash with the Jewish and Roman authorities, his disciples had managed to get hold of a couple of swords.

The fact that Luke mentions only one zealot could imply that the remainder of Jesus' twelve disciples were a little more relaxed about the foreign occupants or, at least, unwilling to fight them. But there are hints in the Gospels that Jesus' followers expected him to restore Israel's sovereignty.

While they followed him around during his public ministry, the disciples and the crowds of people heard Jesus talk about the coming kingdom of God, again and again. So was this Passover festival the moment of truth? Jerusalem was packed with ecstatic pilgrims and Roman soldiers on edge; God's temple was the focus of everyone's attention. Could this be the moment for Jesus to declare himself Israel's Messiah – their promised royal leader – and take on the Roman rulers, and for God to miraculously intervene and restore Israel's former glory?

But things turned out rather differently.

WITH FRIENDS
LIKE THESE

At certain points in his public ministry, hundreds, even
thousands gathered around Jesus.

In the end, he was on his own. Arrested by Roman soldiers,
with no one to jump to his defence. How come?

Soon after catching the public eye, Jesus briefly reached
celebrity status. The message of the young preacher and miracle
worker from up north in Galilee had fired people's imaginations.
Who wouldn't want a piece of one who sided with nobodies like
them, healed the chronically ill in an instant and kindled hopes
of Israel taking back control from the Roman invaders?

The common people wanted to meet the miracle worker from
Galilee, because most of them were dirt poor, many of them sick

and none of them keen on armed, tax-hungry Romans.

And so people pushed, shoved and craned their necks as Jesus taught in town squares and on lake shores, fed the hungry, touched lepers, rescued a woman from public execution and got the town villain to give half his fortune to the poor.

Yet, Jesus was unmoved by the adulation. And as people listened closely, it dawned on them that he was not about health, wealth and 'happy ever after'. He said unsettling things about loving your enemy, living lives of utter inner purity, and of suffering for his name's sake.

Little wonder that, in the end, the crowds melted away. Even the few blokes and women who stuck with him struggled to grasp that the path he taught them to follow would involve self-denial and sacrifice.

After Jesus' arrest and during his trial, when the disciple named Peter was identified as a Jesus-follower, Peter swore not to know him. You cannot help but wonder, was his denial purely due to fear of being arrested along with Jesus? Or was there also an element of disillusionment because the hope of Messiah Jesus taking over from the Romans hadn't materialised? Not only had he been defeated by the enemy; he hadn't even put up a fight.

Similarly, might Judas, the disciple who has gone down in history as the arch-traitor for leading the soldiers to Jesus, have turned against his master, the moment he realised that Jesus would never pick up a sword to usher in God's rule?

The Bible reports that the disciples stayed with Jesus when the soldiers and Judas arrived but took to their heels as soon as they realised that Jesus was not going to lift a finger against those who had come to arrest him.

No one, it would seem, who encountered Jesus between his first public appearance and his arrest had truly understood what he was about. In the end, they all gave up on him.

BREAD AND WINE

Whether or not you go to church, you'll probably be aware that Communion is often at the heart of the service.

It tends to be a fairly solemn, soul-searching affair. Originally it was more about Christians sharing a meal together, and, going by what we read in the Bible about the church in the Greek city of Corinth, some apparently saw it as a chance to party.

But one thing has remained the same over the centuries. Then and now, bread and wine play a key part. Like Passover for Jews, Communion is a commemorative meal for Christians. Jews remember the rescue from bondage in ancient Egypt. Christians remember the rescue from the bondage of evil and death.

The first Jesus-followers had to accept that his messianic mission hadn't been about national politics. The Romans were still there. In AD70, a few decades after brutally killing Jesus, their armies under General Titus would raze Jerusalem to the ground.

In other words, Jesus had been engaged in a different kind of battle. The biblical accounts of him warring with the devil and his demons may seem outlandish to many modern-day readers, but they point right to the heart of the matter: he was acting on behalf of God by taking on the forces of evil that were opposed to God and destroying people's lives.

The Communion bread and wine speak of his struggle with evil reaching its climax. They symbolise his body and blood. He used that imagery himself while celebrating the Passover meal with his friends on the eve of his crucifixion.

The early church came to recognise that Jesus was a suffering Messiah who had voluntarily taken human evil and misery upon himself. The Greeks and Romans told stories of gods that were fickle, jealous, scheming, aloof. In Christ crucified, his followers discovered a God who was vulnerable and compassionate.

Jesus, the Son of God, had fought a battle, not against foreign oppressors, but of light against darkness, of love against hate. Yet as he hung there on a cross crying out, 'My God, why have you forsaken me?' he looked well and truly beaten.

MARY, QUITE CONTRARY

Back in 1948, when an unsuspecting farmer and his brothers dug around a boulder near the Egyptian town of Nag Hammadi and hit upon a tall earthenware jar, they were unaware that it contained a stack of 1600-year-old writings.

One of the ancient manuscripts describes the rather close friendship between Jesus and Mary Magdalene. This sparked some weird and wonderful theories, including one that might be on your bookshelf: Dan Brown's *Da Vinci Code*.

Sadly for romantically inclined conspiracy theorists, the old papyrus known as the Gospel of Philip was composed a few hundred years after Jesus was born. It is heavily influenced by a non-Christian religion called Gnosticism and describes the relationship between Jesus and Mary essentially in platonic terms.

Philip's famous, apparently juicy passage about Jesus kissing

Mary on her lips is a fragment with the decisive words actually missing, so the translation of what the original might have said is guesswork.

The Gospel of Philip is one of several so-called apocryphal Gospels that didn't make it into the Bible, because they portray a Gnostic rather than a Jewish Jesus. Gnostics believed in redemption from our earthly lot by spiritual insight – the 'divine spark' as they called it. Jesus taught redemption by the grace of God. These apocryphal writings were written much later than our so-called canonical Gospels – Matthew, Mark, Luke and John – which were all penned by the end of the first century, at a time when people who had met either Jesus or an eyewitness of the events were still alive and could be questioned.

The four Gospels agree that three days after Jesus' crucifixion his tomb was found empty. Three of them add sightings of the risen Christ, and in John's Gospel Mary Magdalene appears as a key witness. But Mary, quite contrary to what the third-century manuscript from Nag Hammadi would have us believe, is neither Jesus' girlfriend nor his favourite disciple. She is one of several female followers who discover the empty tomb on Easter Sunday.

John touchingly describes Mary being in tears and trying to hold on to Jesus, once she has recognised him standing outside the tomb. More importantly for our purposes, this short Gospel passage holds some vital clues to the resurrection.

Firstly, Jesus' followers didn't have grief-induced hallucinatory visions, as is sometimes suggested. Finding the tomb empty, Mary suspects grave robbery and initially mistakes Jesus for the gardener. She needs some persuading to believe it is him.

Secondly, like Mary Magdalene, Jesus' male disciples didn't expect him to return from the grave. According to their theology, God might simultaneously bring *all* his faithful departed to life at the end of time; bumping into a risen Jesus there and then wasn't part of the plan.

Thirdly, Mary takes a while to recognise Jesus. He seems both different and the same. He appears in what Paul, the great missionary of the early church, thinks of as a spiritual, glorified body. He is no ghost, as Mary is able to cling to him, but he is different, nonetheless. It is as if heaven and earth had touched and merged on Easter morning.

Fourthly, Christ appears to a woman, whose witness had no

weight in those days. Why would John, who wanted to convince his readers that Jesus was the risen Son of God, highlight a woman's encounter with him unless it had happened?

Finally, Jesus tells Mary to go and tell the disciples. What, other than encountering the risen Christ, would have filled her and others with the desire and courage to proclaim an executed Messiah to a sceptical and hostile audience? As Paul put it, 'We proclaim Christ crucified, a stumbling-block to Jews and foolishness to Gentiles.' They did so, because they had seen him not only dead but alive.

END OF THE ROAD?

Mary Magdalene's encounter with the risen Christ, then, corrects some popular misconceptions about what resurrection is and what it isn't. But one thing the passage in John's Gospel doesn't address is the deeply ingrained Jewish view that the Messiah was meant to restore Israel's former glory; so it's time to turn to another resurrection story, in the Gospel of Luke.

On the first Easter Sunday afternoon, two of Jesus' followers are walking towards a village called Emmaus, near Jerusalem, when they are joined by the risen Jesus. Like Mary Magdalene, they fail to recognise him. Funnily enough, they tell him the whole story about what happened to him on Good Friday.

Good Friday had shattered their dreams. All was lost. It was time to go home to Emmaus – or wherever, just as long as it was away from Jerusalem. Bolt the doors and keep their heads down, in case some zealous priest or suspicious soldier tried to stamp out what was left of the Jesus movement. Emmaus must literally have felt like the end of the road.

Arriving at their village, the two friends have the bright idea of inviting the stranger to dinner. He breaks the bread, their eyes are opened, and at last they recognise him.

While still on the road to Emmaus, the friends remarked, 'But we had hoped that he was the one to redeem Israel.' Here we have it again: the expectation of a triumphant, political Messiah. Jesus argues that if they had read the Scriptures carefully, they would have realised that the Messiah was predicted to suffer.

We saw earlier that Jesus' earthly mission was first and foremost spiritual; and yet, his resurrection ended up having considerable political implications.

Firstly, the powers of the world had been unable to stop him. Caiaphas and Pilate had conspired to kill him; God had brought him back to life.

Moreover, the early Christians went on to proclaim Jesus, not as a good moral teacher but as Messiah, Son of God and Saviour. Loyalty to him trumped loyalty to earthly rulers, especially if they expected to be treated like divinity. Loyalty to him also trumped loyalty to the family or city gods; you couldn't just add Jesus to the pantheon of deities that everyone else was worshipping.

To declare Jesus as Lord was such an exclusive stance that it set Christians on a collision course with relatives, neighbours, priests and government officials. To claim that Jesus Christ was not only Israel's redeemer but Lord of the world was simply outrageous. If Emperor Claudius really did pick up rumours about a risen Son of God and decide on a precautionary decree, we shouldn't be too surprised.

When all is said and done, the resurrection message is good news – which is what the word 'Gospel' means. Encountering Jesus at Emmaus turned the two friends' despair to joy.

Resurrection stories may still fly in the face of human experience and reason. But as we said at the outset, why should this be impossible for God? Provided he exists. Provided he intervenes. Provided he is a God of love. The Gospel message that has been proclaimed since the first Easter invites us to trust him with our lives, and to recognise his son, Jesus, alive and walking with us, all the way to the end of the road.

LIKE TO KNOW MORE ... ?

On the remaining pages of this book, you will find the story of Jesus' death and resurrection, taken from the Gospels of Mark, Luke and John. If you would like to know more about what Jesus said and did before his crucifixion, his whole story is told in the four Gospels (Matthew, Mark, Luke and John), which are the first books in the New Testament section of the Bible.

On the Bible Society website, you can find a pocket-sized edition of the Gospels (in the New Revised Standard Version of the Bible): biblesociety.org.uk/pocketgospels

If you would like a copy of the whole Bible, try this pocket-sized edition of the Good News Bible: biblesociety.org.uk/compactgnb

The crucifixion of Jesus in Mark's Gospel
Mark 15

Pilate questions Jesus

Early the next morning the chief priests, the nation's leaders, and the teachers of the Law of Moses met together with the whole Jewish council. They tied up Jesus and led him off to Pilate.

He asked Jesus, 'Are you the king of the Jews?'

'Those are your words,' Jesus answered.

The chief priests brought many charges against Jesus. Then Pilate questioned him again, 'Don't you have anything to say? Don't you hear what crimes they say you have done?' But Jesus did not answer, and Pilate was amazed.

The death sentence

During Passover, Pilate always freed one prisoner chosen by the people. And at that time there was a prisoner named Barabbas. He and some others had been arrested for murder during a riot. The crowd now came and asked Pilate to set a prisoner free, just as he usually did.

Pilate asked them, 'Do you want me to free the king of the Jews?'

Pilate knew that the chief priests had brought Jesus to him because they were jealous.

But the chief priests told the crowd to ask Pilate to free Barabbas.

Then Pilate asked the crowd, 'What do you want me to do with this man you say is the king of the Jews?'

They yelled, 'Nail him to a cross!'

Pilate asked, 'But what crime has he done?'

'Nail him to a cross!' they yelled even louder.

Pilate wanted to please the crowd. So he set Barabbas free. Then he ordered his soldiers to beat Jesus with a whip and nail him to a cross.

Soldiers make fun of Jesus

The soldiers led Jesus inside the courtyard of the fortress and called together the rest of the troops. They put a purple robe on him, and on his head they placed a crown that they had made out of thorn branches. They made fun of Jesus and shouted, 'Hey, you king of the Jews!' Then they beat him on the head with a stick. They spat on him and knelt down and pretended to worship him.

When the soldiers had finished making fun of Jesus, they took off the purple robe. They put his own clothes back on him and led him off to be nailed to a cross. Simon from Cyrene happened to be coming in from a farm, and they forced him to carry Jesus' cross. Simon was the father of Alexander and Rufus.

Jesus is nailed to a cross

The soldiers took Jesus to Golgotha, which means 'Place of a Skull'. There they gave him some wine mixed with a drug to ease the pain, but he refused to drink it.

They nailed Jesus to a cross and gambled to see who would get his clothes. It was about nine o'clock in the morning when they nailed him to the cross. On it was a sign that told why he was nailed there. It read, 'This is the King of the Jews'. The soldiers also nailed two criminals on crosses, one to the right of Jesus and the other to his left.

People who passed by said terrible things about Jesus. They shook their heads and shouted, 'Ha! So you're the one who claimed you could tear down the temple and build it again in three days. Save yourself and come down from the cross!'

The chief priests and the teachers of the Law of Moses also made fun of Jesus. They said to each other, 'He saved others, but he can't save himself. If he is the Messiah, the king of Israel, let him come down from the cross! Then we will see and believe.' The two criminals also said cruel things to Jesus.

The death of Jesus

About noon the sky turned dark and stayed that way until around three o'clock. Then about that time Jesus shouted, 'Eloi, Eloi, sabachthani?' which means, 'My God, my God, why have you deserted me?'

Some of the people standing there heard Jesus and said, 'He is calling for Elijah.' One of them ran and grabbed a sponge. After he had soaked it in wine, he put it on a stick and held it up to Jesus. He said, 'Let's wait and see if Elijah will come and take him down!' Jesus shouted and then died.

At once the curtain in the temple tore in two from top to bottom.

A Roman army officer was standing in front of Jesus. When the officer saw how Jesus died, he said, 'This man really was the Son of God!'

Some women were looking on from a distance. They had come with Jesus to Jerusalem. But even before this they had been his followers and had helped him while he was in Galilee. Mary Magdalene and Mary the mother of the younger James and of Joseph were two of these women. Salome was also one of them.

Jesus is buried

It was now the evening before the Sabbath, and the Jewish people were getting ready for that sacred day. A man named Joseph from Arimathea was brave enough to ask Pilate for the body of Jesus. Joseph was a highly respected member of the Jewish council, and he was also waiting for God's kingdom to come.

Pilate was surprised to hear that Jesus was already dead, and he called in the army officer to find out if Jesus had been dead very long. After the officer told him, Pilate let Joseph have Jesus' body.

Joseph bought a linen cloth and took the body down from the cross. He had it wrapped in the cloth, and he put it in a tomb that had been cut into solid rock. Then he rolled a big stone against the entrance to the tomb.

Mary Magdalene and Mary the mother of Joseph were watching and saw where the body was placed.

Encounter with Jesus on the road to Emmaus
Luke 24.13–35

That same day two of Jesus' disciples were going to the village of
Emmaus, which was about seven miles from Jerusalem. As they were
talking and thinking about what had happened, Jesus came near and
started walking along beside them. But they did not know who he was.

Jesus asked them, 'What were you talking about as you walked
along?'

The two of them stood there looking sad and gloomy. Then the one
named Cleopas asked Jesus, 'Are you the only person from Jerusalem
who didn't know what was happening there these last few days?'

'What do you mean?' Jesus asked.

They answered:

Those things that happened to Jesus from Nazareth. By what he
did and said he showed that he was a powerful prophet, who pleased
God and all the people. Then the chief priests and our leaders had him
arrested and sentenced to die on a cross. We had hoped that he would
be the one to set Israel free! But it has already been three days since all
this happened.

Some women in our group surprised us. They had gone to the tomb early in the morning, but did not find the body of Jesus. They came back, saying that they had seen a vision of angels who told them that he is alive. Some men from our group went to the tomb and found it just as the women had said. But they didn't see Jesus either.

Then Jesus asked the two disciples, 'Why can't you understand? How can you be so slow to believe all that the prophets said? Didn't you know that the Messiah would have to suffer before he was given his glory?' Jesus then explained everything written about himself in the Scriptures, beginning with the Law of Moses and the Books of the Prophets.

When the two of them came near the village where they were going, Jesus seemed to be going farther. They begged him, 'Stay with us! It's already late, and the sun is going down.' So Jesus went into the house to stay with them.

After Jesus sat down to eat, he took some bread. He blessed it and broke it. Then he gave it to them. At once they knew who he was, but he disappeared. They said to each other, 'When he talked with us along the road and explained the Scriptures to us, didn't it warm our hearts?' So they got right up and returned to Jerusalem.

The two disciples found the eleven apostles and the others gathered together. And they learned from the group that the Lord was really alive and had appeared to Peter. Then the disciples from Emmaus told what happened on the road and how they knew he was the Lord when he broke the bread.

Mary Magdalene encounters the risen Jesus
John 20.11–18

Mary Magdalene stood crying outside the tomb. She was still weeping, when she stooped down and saw two angels inside. They were dressed in white and were sitting where Jesus' body had been. One was at the head and the other was at the foot. The angels asked Mary, 'Why are you crying?'

She answered, 'They have taken away my Lord's body! I don't know where they have put him.'

As soon as Mary said this, she turned around and saw Jesus standing there. But she did not know who he was. Jesus asked her, 'Why are you crying? Who are you looking for?'

She thought he was the gardener and said, 'Sir, if you have taken his body away, please tell me, so I can go and get him.'

Then Jesus said to her, 'Mary!'

She turned and said to him, 'Rabboni.' The Aramaic word 'Rabboni' means 'Teacher'.

Jesus told her, 'Don't hold on to me! I have not yet gone to the Father. But tell my disciples that I am going to the one who is my Father and my God, as well as your Father and your God.' Mary Magdalene then went and told the disciples that she had seen the Lord. She also told them what he had said to her.